MW01043163

Science Links

Blood

SUSAN RING

CHELSEA CLUBHOUSE

An Imprint of Chelsea House Publishers

A Haights Cross Communications Company

Philadelphia

This edition first published in 2003 by Chelsea Clubhouse, a division of
Chelsea House Publishers and a subsidiary of Haights Cross Communications.

A Haights Cross Communications ➤ Company

This edition was adapted from Newbridge Discovery Links® by arrangement with Newbridge Educational Publishing.
All rights reserved. No part of this publication may be reproduced or transmitted in any form or by any means without
the written permission of the publisher. Printed and bound in the United States of America.

Chelsea Clubhouse
1974 Sproul Road, Suite 400
Broomall, PA 19008-0914

The Chelsea House world wide web address is www.chelseahouse.com

Library of Congress Cataloging-in-Publication Data
Ring, Susan.
  Blood / by Susan Ring.
      p. cm. — (Science links)
Includes index.
Contents: A life force — The body's delivery system — The body's defenders — A sticky situation — New blood.
  ISBN 0-7910-7418-8
  1. Blood—Juvenile literature. [1. Blood.] I. Title. II. Series.
  QP91 .R565 2003
  612.1'1—dc21

                                                                          2002015900

Copyright © Newbridge Educational Publishing LLC

Newbridge Discovery Links Guided Reading Program Author: Dr. Brenda Parkes
Content Reviewer: Burton Fletcher, M.D., Brooklyn, NY
Written by Susan Ring

Cover Photograph: A close-up view of blood cells
Table of Contents Photograph: Blood transfusion under way during surgery

Photo Credits:
Cover: National Cancer Institute/Science Photo Library; Table of Contents page: Barry Slaven/Visuals Unlimited, Inc.;
pages 4-5: Jim Cummins/The Stock Market/CORBIS; page 6: Mark E. Gibson/Visuals Unlimited, Inc.; page 7: Visuals
Unlimited, Inc.; page 9: Martin Wendler/Okapia/Photo Researchers, Inc.; page 10: (top) J.H. Robinson/Photo
Researchers, Inc., (bottom) Andrew G. Wood/Photo Researchers, Inc.; page 11: David Wrobel/Visuals Unlimited, Inc.;
pages 12-13: SCIMAT/Photo Researchers, Inc.; page 14: Meckes/Ottawa/Photo Researchers, Inc.; page 15: Digital
Imagery © copyright 2001 Photodisc, Inc.; pages 16-17: Dr. Arnold Brody/SPL/Photo Researchers, Inc.; page 18:
Bettmann/CORBIS; page 19: (background) Robert Franz/CORBIS, (inset) Kent Wood/Photo Researchers, Inc.; pages
20-21: David M. Phillips/Visuals Unlimited, Inc.; page 22: (all photos) Erich Schrempp/Photo Researchers, Inc.; page
23: Gunter Ziesler/Peter Arnold, Inc.; pages 24-25: Barry Slaven/Visuals Unlimited, Inc.; page 27: The American Red
Cross; page 29: Prof. P. Motta/Dept. of Anatomy/University of "La Sapienza," Rome/SPL/Photo Researchers, Inc.

Illustrations by Barb Cousins, pages 8, 26, 28

While every care has been taken to trace and acknowledge photo copyrights for this edition, the publisher apologizes
for any accidental infringement where copyright has proved untraceable.

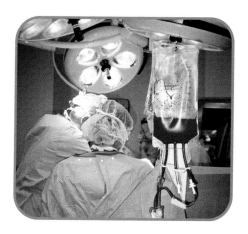

Table of Contents

A Life Force

Whether you are playing ball or sitting and reading a book, blood is flowing through your body. Blood is a life force that keeps your body working. Without it, you could not survive.

If you have ever fallen and scraped your knee, you have seen your blood. This bright red liquid doesn't look very important. So why do we need it? What does blood do? What is blood made of, and how do its different parts work to keep your body healthy?

Get ready to take a closer look at this amazing life force.

The amount of blood in a person's body depends upon the person's size. A 160-pound (73-kilogram) adult has about 5 quarts (4.7 liters) of blood, an 80-pound (36-kilogram) child has about half this amount, and a newborn baby has only about 10 ounces (293 milliliters) of blood.

Going with the Flow

Your body is made up of many different kinds of cells. For example, your brain is made up of brain cells, and your muscles are made up of muscle cells. All of your cells need blood to survive!

Probably the most important jobs that blood performs are to deliver oxygen and food to cells throughout your body and to take waste products away from the cells. Blood also helps keep your body temperature steady, whether you are out sledding in the snow or playing ball on a summer day.

The average body temperature for a healthy human being is 98.6 degrees Fahrenheit (37 degrees celsius), even when the temperature outside dips to below freezing.

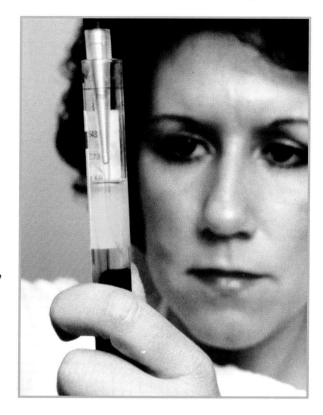

When blood sits in a test tube, the yellowish plasma will rise to the top, and the other parts of the blood will sink to the bottom.

To do its many jobs, blood contains different kinds of cells, each of which performs specific functions. These cells float in a liquid called **plasma**. Plasma is mostly water. It is like a river that travels through your body, carrying the blood cells along. But this river must follow a certain route to make sure that your blood keeps moving in just the right way.

Blood on the Move

Blood gets to your heart and brain, and around the rest of your body, by traveling through the many tiny tubes that make up the circulatory system. Your body has millions of tubes called **blood vessels**. These blood vessels transport your blood. Different blood vessels do different things.

Arteries carry oxygen-filled blood away from your heart and lungs and deliver it to cells throughout your body. Blood flowing through your body also includes nutrients that give energy to your cells and keep them healthy.

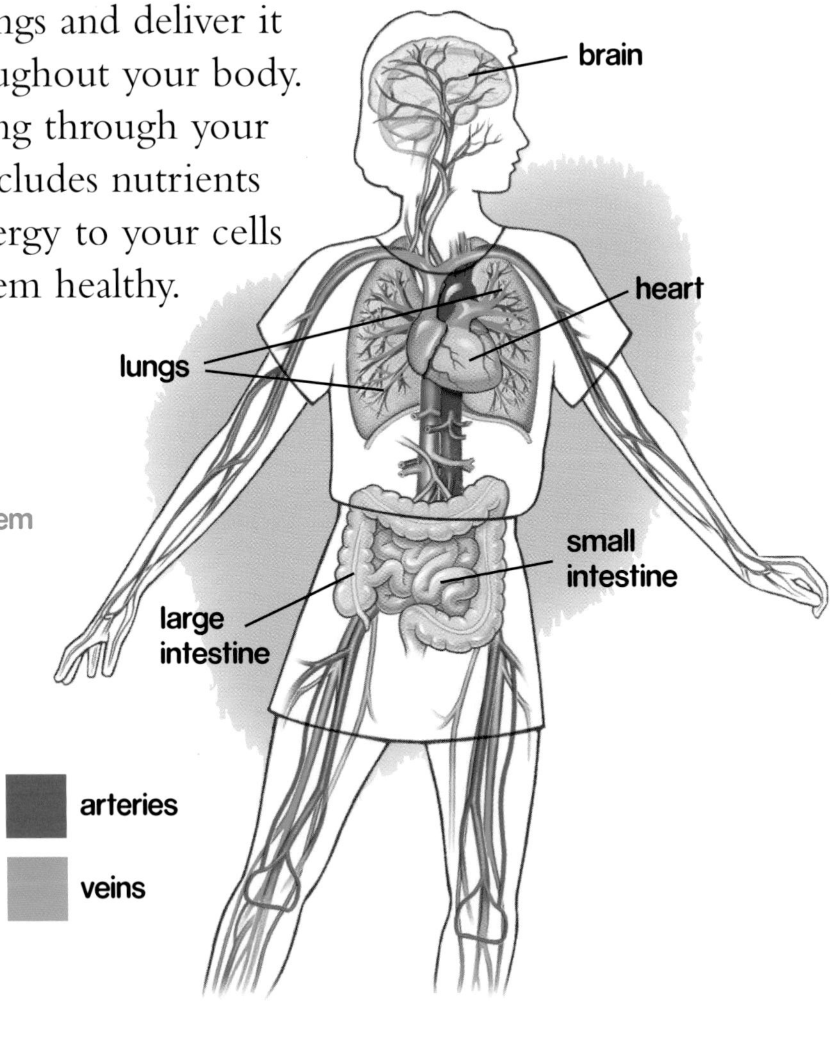

brain

heart

lungs

Diagram of the circulatory system

small intestine

large intestine

arteries

veins

Insects have only one blood vessel. So how does blood travel around their bodies? An insect's blood flows through that one blood vessel and into the hollow spaces that reach up to its head, and all the way down through its legs, and out to its antennae and wings.

After the blood has delivered the oxygen and nutrients, other blood vessels called **veins** bring the blood back to your heart and lungs. Veins also carry waste materials away from your cells. In order to reach every part of your body, veins and arteries branch out into smaller and smaller vessels. The tiniest of these are called **capillaries**. Capillaries are so small and thin that nutrients pass right through their walls.

The heart is a muscle that pumps blood, and it's one of the hardest-working organs in your body. In one person's average lifetime, the heart will beat more than 2.5 billion times. It's so strong that it can pump a drop of blood around your body in less than a minute. And that's a greater distance than you might think. Each person has about 100,000 miles (160,930 kilometers) of blood vessels!

A Colorful Fluid

All blood serves the same purpose. But not all blood looks the same. Some animals have blood that is blue, yellow, or even green! Lobsters and crabs have blue blood because their blood contains copper. Starfish have clear or yellowish blood. Earthworms and leeches have a substance in their blood that makes it green. Some insects have yellow or green blood because of the color of the plants they eat. And sea anemones have no blood at all!

How do sea anemones live without blood? Seawater passes in and out of their bodies,

Starfish

Lobster

carrying nutrients and removing wastes, in much the same way blood performs these functions for other animals.

Of course, human blood is red. That's because it is filled with special cells called red blood cells that contain a bright red substance called **hemoglobin**.

Sea Anemone

The Body's Delivery System

No, these perfectly shaped red disks are not flying saucers! This picture shows what hemoglobin-rich, red blood cells look like when viewed through a microscope. The shape of these cells helps them bend, twist, and turn through the tiniest blood vessels without getting stuck.

Red blood cells are like delivery trucks that begin at the heart, then make their first stop at the lungs. The hemoglobin they contain allows them to pick up the oxygen you breathe in. Then they go back to the heart and deliver the oxygen to the cells throughout your body. After they unload the oxygen, they pick up carbon dioxide from these cells and carry it to your heart and then to your lungs for you to breathe out. After that, the red blood cells circulate back to the heart and begin their trip all over again.

Along the way, blood picks up nutrients from digested food in the intestines. It carries the nutrients to cells all around the body. The red blood cells then deliver oxygen to combine with these nutrients to make energy. This is how you get the energy to bike, or walk, or even blink your eyes.

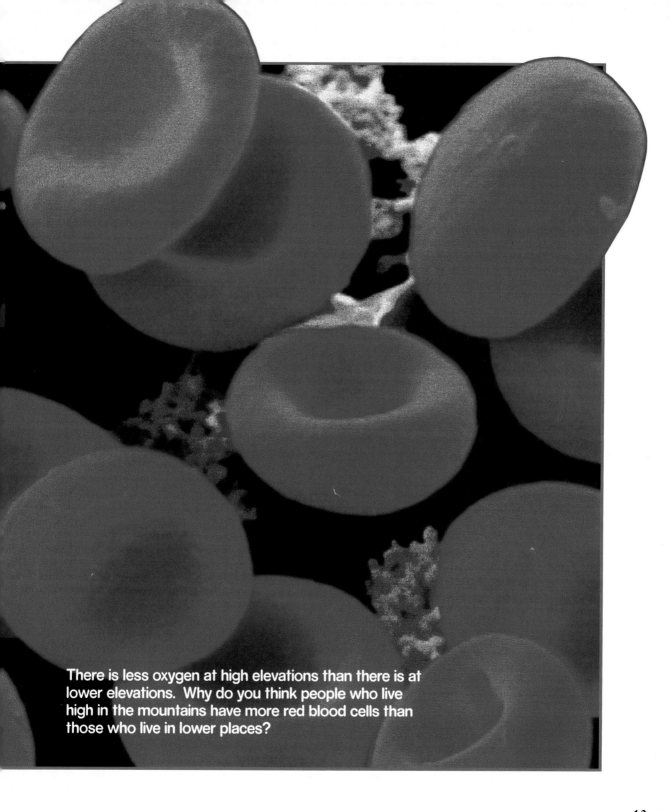

There is less oxygen at high elevations than there is at lower elevations. Why do you think people who live high in the mountains have more red blood cells than those who live in lower places?

Building Better Cells

Each red blood cell should be shaped like a disk in order to bend and twist its way through the blood vessels. But sometimes people are born with a blood disease that makes their red blood cells become crescent shaped. The crescent shape prevents the red blood cells from squeezing through small capillaries to deliver enough oxygen. This disease is called sickle-cell anemia.

Scientists are developing ways to help people with sickle-cell anemia. New drugs are being tested to change the shape of the sickle cell so it can move more easily through the blood vessels.

Another less serious type of **anemia** occurs when a person doesn't have enough red blood cells. Since these cells are the oxygen transporters, having too few means that not enough oxygen is getting to the cells in the body. This can make a person weak and pale.

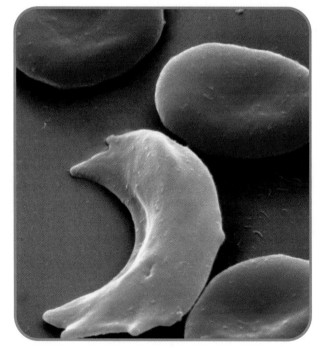

A person with sickle-cell anemia has some normal red blood cells and some damaged ones.

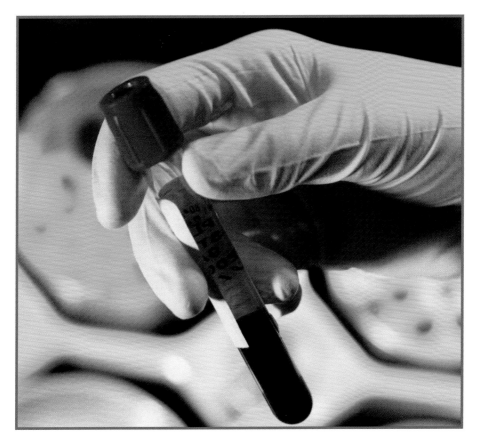

Scientists are working to find new ways to treat
sickle-cell anemia and other blood diseases.

Anemia can usually be prevented or corrected by
eating a diet rich in foods that contain iron, such as
spinach and other leafy vegetables, dried fruit, beans,
red meat, and whole grains. The body uses iron to
make hemoglobin.

Red blood cells do a very important job inside
your body. But your blood also has other types of
cells that work hard to keep you healthy.

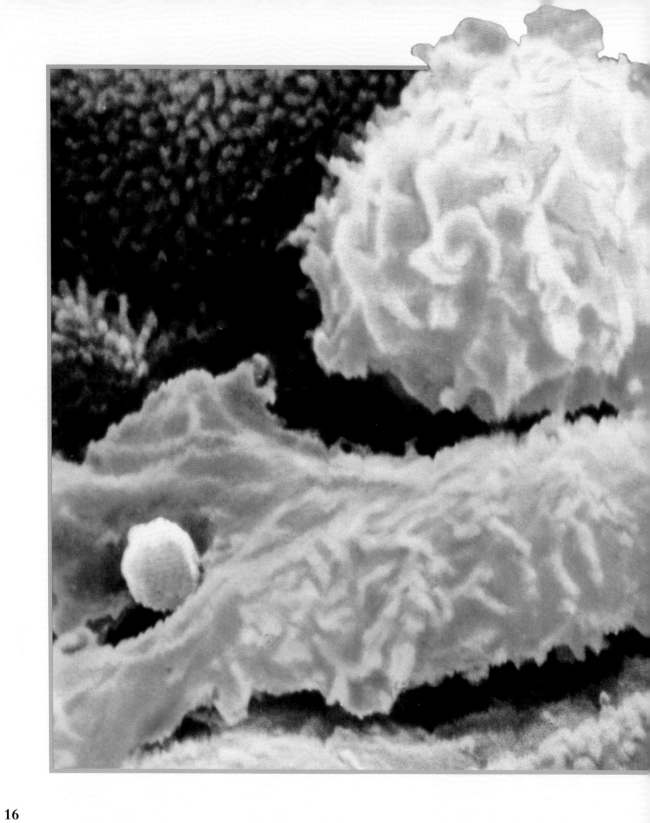

The Body's Defenders

Shifting shape allows white blood cells to move quickly when they surround and attack germs.

The body's white blood cells are always looking for invaders that may cause sickness or infection. When the white blood cells spot an invader, they attack!

There are a few different types of white blood cells. White blood cells called **lymphocytes** battle infections by forming **antibodies**. An antibody will lock onto germs—either viruses, like the ones that cause you to get a cold, or bacteria that might start an infection. Then another white blood cell, called a **macrophage**, will surround the invader and destroy it. In this picture, the round green organism is a germ. It is being surrounded and attacked by a macrophage. The round white cell is a lymphocyte.

Fighting the Enemy

Some white blood cells remember their enemy and will store the matching antibodies just in case the invader comes back again. That's why some diseases, such as chicken pox, infect a person only once. It's also why children are vaccinated against certain diseases. By receiving a weakened or dead form of the germ through a vaccine, the body is tricked into creating enough antibodies to protect itself from ever getting the disease.

Scientists are experimenting with a vaccine for malaria, which is a deadly disease spread by mosquitoes.

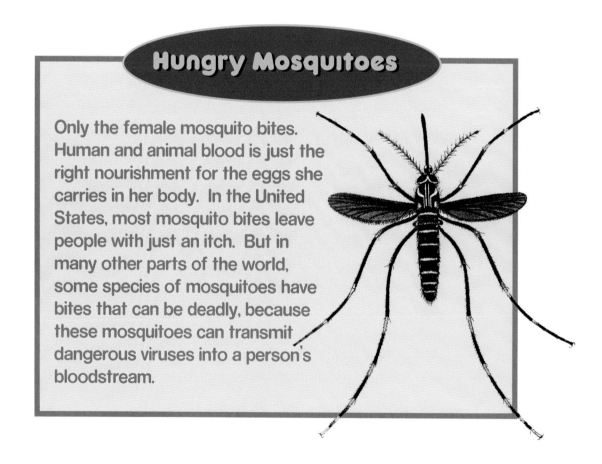

Hungry Mosquitoes

Only the female mosquito bites. Human and animal blood is just the right nourishment for the eggs she carries in her body. In the United States, most mosquito bites leave people with just an itch. But in many other parts of the world, some species of mosquitoes have bites that can be deadly, because these mosquitoes can transmit dangerous viruses into a person's bloodstream.

The deer tick carries Lyme disease. The tick lives in grassy areas and gets its name because it often feeds on the blood of deer.

Ticks also spread diseases. One bite from a tiny deer tick can cause a serious illness called Lyme disease. It can make a person very tired and cause pain in the joints and muscles. Now a vaccine can help protect against Lyme disease, even if a tick takes a bite.

But some diseases can outsmart the white blood cells. These diseases prevent the white blood cells from finding the right antibody to fight them. It is clear that the more doctors know about white blood cells and how they fight disease, the closer they will come to preventing and treating many illnesses.

A Sticky Situation

The lacy web shown here gives you a supersized glimpse into how another important blood component does its work. When you cut your finger or scrape your knee, the bleeding usually stops very soon. That's because the **platelets**, the smallest blood cells, are doing their job. Platelets are colorless, sticky cells. They keep bleeding in check and help to heal your wounds. When you get a cut, your blood is exposed to air. The air alerts your platelets to jump into action. They clump together and start to plug up the cut and trigger the formation of a web of threads called **fibrin**.

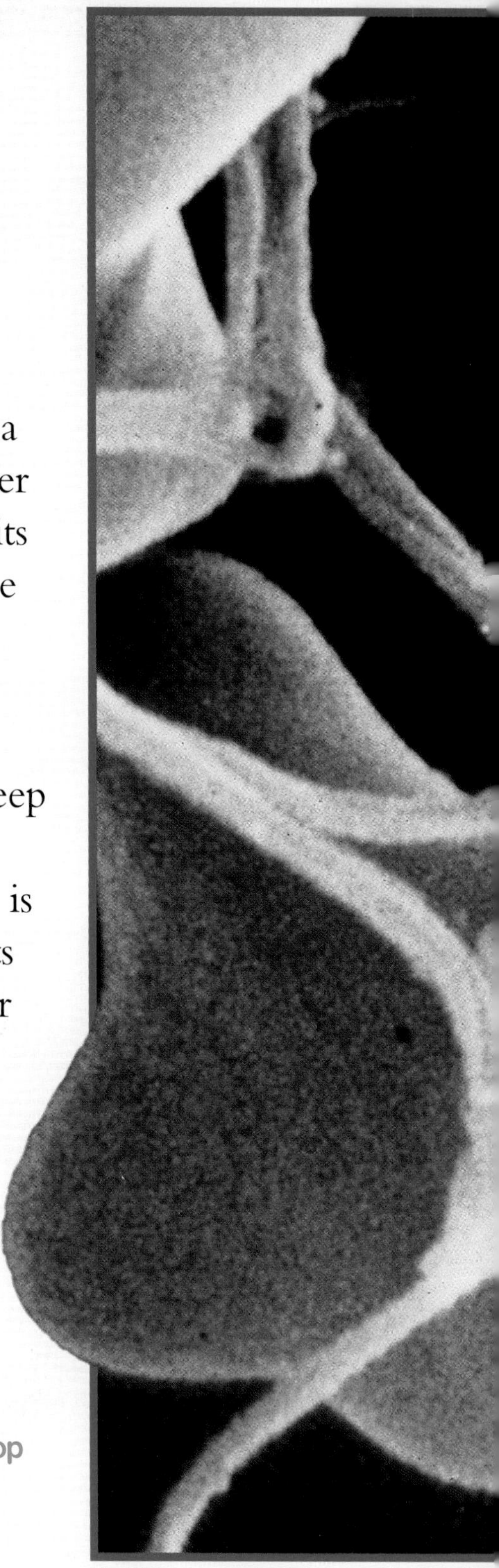

Platelets form a sticky web to stop a cut from bleeding.

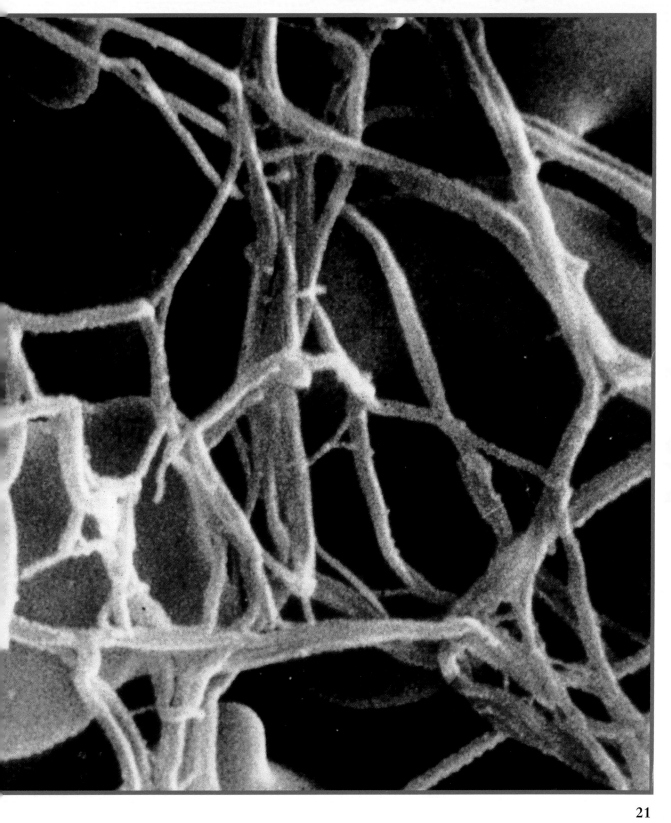

How a Cut Heals:

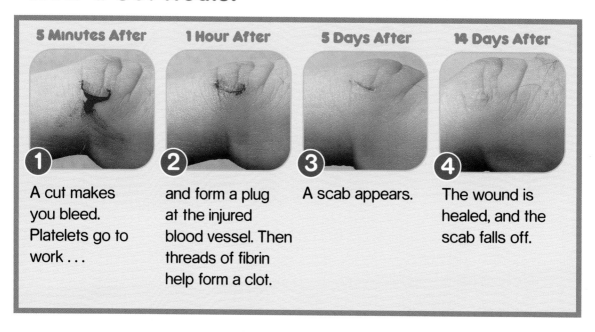

5 Minutes After

1 A cut makes you bleed. Platelets go to work . . .

1 Hour After

2 and form a plug at the injured blood vessel. Then threads of fibrin help form a clot.

5 Days After

3 A scab appears.

14 Days After

4 The wound is healed, and the scab falls off.

Clotting Helps Heal

As these threads of fibrin harden, they trap plasma and red and white blood cells, and form a clot. After the blood dries, a scab forms. In time, the scab dries up and falls off.

Bruises are caused by broken blood vessels and bleeding under your skin. Platelets also stop this kind of bleeding.

Some people are born with a blood disease called hemophilia. This condition occurs when one of the elements that helps blood to clot is reduced. As a result, a person with hemophilia bleeds longer and bruises more easily than other people. One way hemophiliacs cope with their disease is by receiving a special injection. The injection contains the clotting element that is reduced from their blood.

These injections help people with hemophilia to lead more active lives. Scientists are looking for new ways to cure and treat hemophilia. One possibility is to find out how the body can produce more of the clotting element that is reduced.

MEET A VAMPIRE!

Vampire bats have very sharp teeth that they use to make a small hole in an animal's skin. The bat feeds on the animal's blood for about half an hour. Why doesn't the blood clot? As the bat sips the blood, it also sends out saliva which contains a special ingredient that prevents blood from clotting. Vampire bats prefer to eat blood from livestock, and rarely go after humans. A 2-inch (5-centimeter) vampire bat eats only about 1 teaspoon (5 milliters) of blood at a time. Often, the host animal doesn't even know it's there!

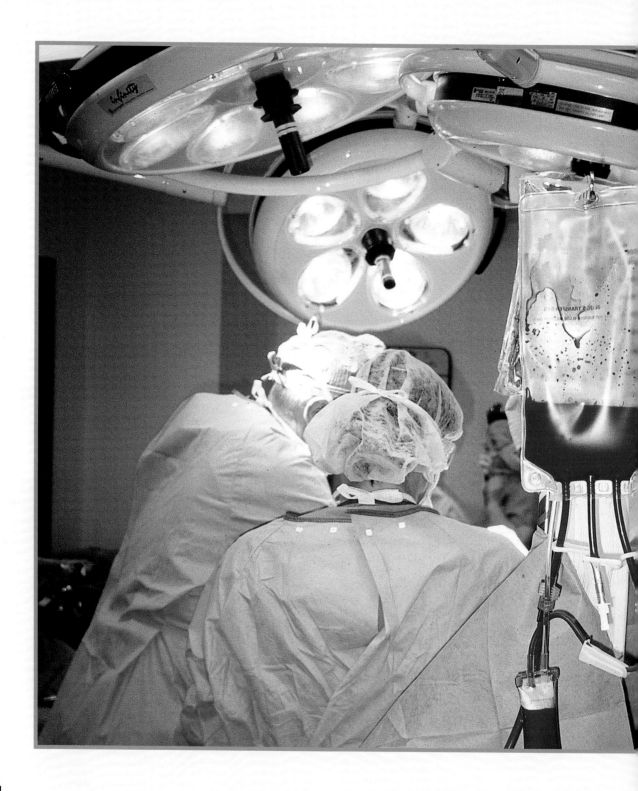

New Blood

Sometimes, people lose a lot of blood in an accident or during an operation. Other times they might have blood that isn't healthy enough to do its job. These people can receive healthy blood from donors who volunteer to give it. This is called a **blood transfusion**. A blood transfusion takes the blood from one person and puts it into the bloodstream of another. Transfusions can save many lives. But in the past a lot of people got sick or died from transfusions. No one knew why until one scientist made a major discovery.

More than 100 years ago, Karl Landsteiner discovered that even though all human blood looks the same, not everyone's blood is alike. He found that blood contains substances called **antigens**. Landsteiner discovered that each person is born with one of four types of antigens: type A, B, AB, or O.

A patient may receive one or several blood transfusions during an operation.

Matching Types for Transfusion

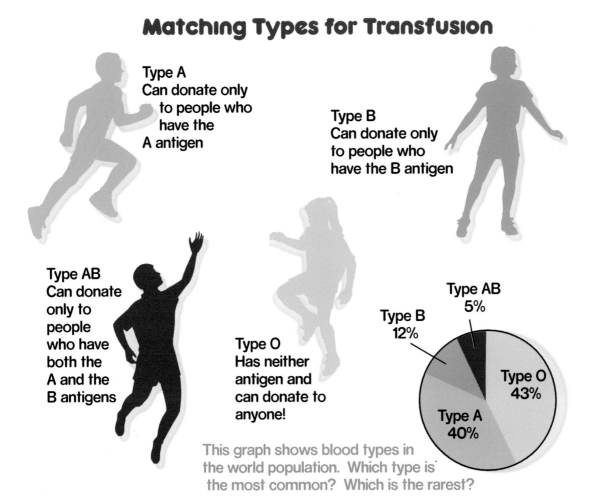

Type A
Can donate only
   to people who
   have the
A antigen

Type B
Can donate only
to people who
have the B antigen

Type AB
Can donate
only to
people
who have
both the
A and the
B antigens

Type O
Has neither
antigen and
can donate to
anyone!

Type AB
5%

Type B
12%

Type O
43%

Type A
40%

This graph shows blood types in
the world population. Which type is
the most common? Which is the rarest?

What's Your Type?

Some antigens can be harmful when added to blood
that doesn't have matching antigens. If a person with
type A blood receives a transfusion of type B blood, the
blood will clump up and stick together. This will make
the person dangerously sick. Today, before a transfusion,
the donated blood is tested to make sure it matches the
patient's blood. It is also tested to make sure it is free of
any disease-carrying viruses or bacteria.

A Special Gift

People volunteer to donate their blood for a blood transfusion. Besides using every element in the blood, doctors can remove just the parts of the blood that a patient needs. This way, patients can receive just plasma, or red cells, or platelets. Blood is collected, tested, and stored at a blood bank until patients need it.

Charles Drew and Blood Banks

In the 1930s, many patients who needed transfusions died because matching blood donors could not be found quickly enough. At that time, whole blood could not be stored longer than ten days. But Dr. Charles Drew knew that plasma could be stored much longer. In the 1940s, during World War II, Dr. Drew found a way to store and ship thousands of pints of much-needed plasma to wounded soldiers. The techniques Dr. Drew developed saved thousands of lives during the war, and led to the kinds of blood banks that are available to help people who need transfusions today.

Blood Factories

Even though some people need to receive blood transfusions, most people never have to worry about replacing lost or worn-out blood cells. New blood cells are always being made and replaced within our bodies. Red blood cells, some white cells, and platelets are made in the **bone marrow**, which is found in the center of bones. The liver releases chemicals that become part of the blood. These help blood to clot, fight infection and build cell walls. Another blood factory is the lymph system. The lymph system makes some of the white blood cells that attack infection. The largest organ in the lymph system is the spleen. It is behind your stomach, and about the size of your heart. Not only does it filter the blood, but it also destroys old, damaged red blood cells and returns the iron back to your bloodstream.

lymph nodes

liver

spleen

bone marrow

Your lymph system, spleen, liver, and the bones in your body are the places where your blood is produced, or manufactured.

This close-up view of bone marrow shows developing red blood cells.

About 100 years ago, doctors realized that some blood diseases were caused by problems in a person's bone marrow. They knew that they could combat such diseases by giving the patient healthy bone marrow from another person. This is called a bone-marrow **transplant**. The first successful bone-marrow transplant was to a boy who was only four months old. Now he is grown-up and has children of his own! Many people all over the world are alive today because of bone-marrow transplants.

And So It Flows

Bone-marrow transplants are just one of the many ways that scientists are trying to help people have healthy blood. Scientists can now manufacture clotting factors, as well as hemoglobin, the red substance that carries oxygen. These developments are certain to save many lives and help people who have problems with their blood. Scientists will continue to study blood because it is such an important life force.

In fact, while you were reading this book, your body was constantly at work, pumping blood, getting rid of old blood cells, making new ones, fighting off disease, and giving you energy. And you didn't even have to think about it to keep this life force flowing!

Websites

Find out more about blood and what it does at these Websites:

sln.fi.edu/biosci/preview/heartpreview.html

kidshealth.org/kid/body/mybody_noSW.html

www.pbs.org/wgbh/nova/eheart

Glossary

anemia: a condition in which blood does not contain enough iron

antibodies: substances made by the blood to fight infection and disease

antigens: chemicals in blood that make it a specific type

arteries: blood vessels that carry blood away from the heart and through the body

blood transfusion: the transfer of blood from one person to another

blood vessels: tubes that carry blood throughout the body

bone marrow: the inner part of a bone in which new blood cells are formed

capillaries: the tiniest blood vessels in the body

fibrin: a web of sticky threads formed by platelets to stop bleeding

hemoglobin: a substance in red blood cells that carries oxygen

lymphocyte: a type of white blood cell that produces antibodies

macrophage: a type of white blood cell that surrounds and destroys invaders

plasma: the watery-liquid part of blood

platelets: tiny cells in the blood that help form clots and stop bleeding

transplant: the act of taking a body part out of one person and putting it in another person

veins: blood vessels that carry blood toward the heart and through the body

Index